Presented to:

Debbie

From:

Joanne

My Sister, My Friend

Nancy Jo Sullivan

Photography by

Kathleen Francour

Multnomah Gifts™
Multnomah® Publishers *Sisters, Oregon*

My Sister, My Friend

©2002 by Nancy Jo Sullivan
published by Multnomah Gifts,™ a division of Multnomah® Publishers, Inc.

ISBN 1-57673-923-6

Artwork © by Kathleen Francour, www.kfrancour.com.

Designed by Koechel Peterson & Associates, Minneapolis, Minnesota

Scripture quotations are taken from *The Holy Bible*, New International Version © 1973, 1984
by International Bible Society, used by permission of Zondervan Publishing House.

Multnomah Publishers, Inc., has made every effort to trace the ownership of all poems and quotes.
In the event of a question arising from the use of a poem or quote, we regret any error made and will be pleased
to make the necessary correction in future editions of this book.

Printed in China

For information:

MULTNOMAH PUBLISHERS, INC.
POST OFFICE BOX 1720
SISTERS, OREGON 97759

02 03 04 05 06 07 08—10 9 8 7 6 5 4 3 2 1 0

www.multnomahgifts.com

Table of Contents

I could never love anyone as I love my sisters.

LOUISA MAY ALCOTT,
SPOKEN BY JO, IN *LITTLE WOMEN*

Introduction

What comes to mind when you think of your sister?

Do you remember your childhood days? The matching dresses you wore on Easter? The hopscotch squares you drew on the sidewalk? The afternoon chats you had in the backyard sandbox?

Perhaps you recall your teenage years. The clothes you borrowed (or stole!) from each other's closets, the fights you had over boyfriends and phone calls and time in the bathroom, or the secrets you told each other just before you fell asleep at night.

Maybe you have mental snapshots of when you were young adults—being in each other's weddings, talking endlessly on the phone about your new jobs, exchanging recipes and diet plans.

Sisters.

While the full meaning of the word is difficult to define, it speaks of a connectedness that is unique—a kinship like no other. You and your sister may share a vibrant relationship that you want to celebrate. Or maybe amid the busyness of life, you long to renew those special ties. Perhaps there is a need for healing, and you desire reconciliation. Each scenario offers a promise of strengthening the special bond of sisterhood.

Truly, the affinity between sisters is a kinship like no other. Revel in its loveliness and intricacies, celebrate priceless memories, and anticipate future joys. Fling open your heart to one of life's sweetest gifts—your sister.

Date Cookies

Bundled in mittens and earmuffs, we rushed home from school, my sister Peggy and I. It was a snowy Friday in January, and our breath froze into frosty puffs. When at last we opened the front door, the familiar aroma of just-baked cookies greeted us.

"Oh no," I whispered. I stomped the snow from my boots.

"She made them again," Peggy groaned, unzipping her jacket.

We looked toward the kitchen. There our grandmother, "Marma," was pulling a sheet of steaming date cookies from the oven. Dressed in a Hawaiian print housedress and fur slippers, she smiled and beckoned us, her pudgy hands covered with pink oven mitts.

"Who wants a treat?" Marma asked.

She held out a plate filled with the heavy, date-laden confections.

Marma was our father's mom. When she came to visit our family, she often stayed for six months at a time. "She has a disease. . .she forgets things. . .be patient with her," my father told us time and time again.

Marma forgot lots of things——our names, the address of our home, where her bedroom was located. So Peggy and I could never figure out how she always remembered an eighty-year-old family recipe that had never been written down. Every afternoon, Marma baked up a fresh batch of date cookies from memory. Peggy and I hated date cookies.

"Thanks," I said, giving Marma a hug.

"Mmm," Peggy added, feigning delight.

I took the plate, and Peggy and I made our way down the hallway to the room we shared. For a moment, we sat on my bed, studying the cookies.

"I can't. . .I can't eat another one," Peggy said.

She picked up the plate of cookies, walked over to the window, and flung it open. I watched as she took aim, and then whirled one of the cookies through the air and into the snow as if she were throwing a Frisbee.

I followed her lead, while the winter wind whooshed snow into our room. I wound up and tossed a cookie with all my might—it hit the neighbors' snow-covered birdbath. We laughed. Peggy sailed another one out the window. We doubled over on my bed with mirth. One by one, we threw every date cookie, giggling uncontrollably as they ricocheted into snow banks and bushes and trees.

Later that night, just before Peggy and I fell asleep, I started to feel guilty.

"If Marma knew, she would be hurt. We wasted food. We committed a sin," I told my sister.

"Just a little sin," Peggy murmured as she dozed off to sleep.

The following afternoon, our family attended confession at our church. I sat on the hard church pew right next to Peggy. I knew that confession required a thorough examination of conscience. Back then receiving pardon for sins was a structured and intimidating experience. I kept fidgeting and tapping my foot.

"Settle down," Peggy whispered.

I watched my sisters and brothers enter a small wooden room, one by one, at the end of our pew. It resembled a telephone booth; the word *Confessional* marked its entrance. When it was my turn, the door closed automatically behind me. The wooden kneeler creaked under my weight. Except for the dim silhouette of the priest on the other side of the small screen, darkness surrounded me.

I took a deep breath. "Father, I've sinned. I threw Marma's cookies in the snow," I said, my hands folded in repentance.

After my confession, I peeked through the screen. I could see the pastor's shoulders shaking as he tried to conceal his laughter. Muted chuckles punctuated his words: "Next time…eat the cookies. It's a sacrifice that will please God," he said.

I came out of the confessional, relieved that it was over. Peggy was making her way to the booth, and when I passed her, I nudged her and whispered, "I told him about the cookies. God forgives us."

After Peggy's turn, the two of us met at the back of the church. We quietly discussed our penance. "We gotta eat 'em," Peggy declared.

For the next two months, Peggy and I ate date cookies every afternoon in our room. In between swallows of dates and oatmeal chunks, we laughed.

We were in this together. It seemed almost fun.

Though I am now a grown woman, I often find myself remembering those winter afternoons that Peggy and I spent eating date cookies. Looking back, I am grateful for the "precious penance" we shared. As sisters, we learned three immutable truths about life: Date cookies taste awful, laughter minimizes sacrifice, and God forgives sins. Even little ones.

You are just as much my sister as when we crouched under the table together, making endless cups of tea for our teddy bears.

PAM BROWN

Bathroom

Wrapped in my powder blue robe, I stood outside the bathroom door, holding my towel and waiting for my turn to brush my teeth. Four of my sisters had been standing in front of the bathroom mirror for two hours, putting on makeup and combing their hair. With just twenty minutes left until my school bus arrived, I could still hear the blow dryer buzzing behind the bathroom door. I pounded on the door. "Hurry up!" I yelled. I pounded again. No response.

I slid down to the carpet and dropped my head to my knees. Still in her footed pajamas, my ten-year-old sister, Annie, plopped down next to me and patted me on the back.

"Someday, I'll have a luxury bathroom," I told her.

Annie's eyes grew wide. She was five years younger than I was, and the only sister who truly looked up to me. She listened intently as I imagined the bathroom of my dreams.

Dreams

"My bathroom will be huge.... It will have a heated tile floor and beautiful curtains and plush towels that hang from gold hooks," I said.

Annie nodded. "When I grow up, I'll have a luxury bathroom too."

Every morning after that, Annie and I sat outside the bathroom, waiting our turn and exchanging extravagant visions.

"My bathroom will have plants and fragrant candles and baskets filled with flowers," I said.

"My bathroom will have shelves filled with bubble bath and soap that smells like strawberries," Annie responded.

We talked about everything from shiny pedestal sinks to peppermint toothpaste. One morning, Annie got carried away. "My bathroom will have a waterproof robot that serves fine food," she said. We laughed.

Now, so many years later, memories of those mornings still linger. These days, Annie and I are busy raising our families. She lives in a modest two-story home with two small bathrooms. So do I. Sometimes we call each other just to dream once again about the luxury bathrooms that will surely be ours... someday.

Sitting and talking in front of the fireplace this past Christmas, we couldn't resist adding more details to the blueprints of our future bathrooms.

"My bathroom will have a skylight," I said.

"Mine will have a built-in sound system," Annie replied.

Her wide grin mirrored mine as we exchanged gifts. I gave Annie a beautifully wrapped package of strawberry-scented soap. She gave me bubble bath trimmed with a red satin bow.

But the sweetest gifts that day were the ones unseen—shared memories and dreams.

We wove a web in childhood, a web of sunny air.
CHARLOTTE BRONTË

Sisters...like coming home again...
She knows just where I've dreamed to go,
remembers where I've been,
accepts me just the way I am—
and treats me like a friend.

She is someone who is there for me,
no matter what or when—
And every time I'm with her
it's like coming home again.

—AUTHOR UNKNOWN

Reflection

My sisters and I rushed downstairs to the rec room to watch *Wheel of Fortune*. We grabbed floor pillows and staked out places to sit, the six of us encircling the TV like a fan. My oldest sister, Jeanne, sixteen at the time, assumed her usual place of prominence in front of the screen. I sat right next to her.

The game show began, and as soon as the beautiful host greeted the TV audience, Jeanne flipped her long blond hair and opened her makeup trunk. Inside were curlers and cosmetics and creams. At fourteen, I was enchanted by her trunk of treasures. I watched her pull a comb from the box and begin to roll her long locks around huge curlers that looked like giant orange juice cans.

Jeanne set her hair in front of the TV every night, and my sisters were getting tired of it. "You're blocking our view," they told her. "Get out of the way!"

Jeanne misted her bangs with hairspray. "I can do whatever I want," she replied.

My sisters may have been disgusted with Jeanne, but I strained to see her reflection in the mirror that lined the lid of the trunk. She's so beautiful, I said to myself, not at all like me. I had short dark hair, with bangs that stuck out above my eyebrows. I was skinny and my teeth were crooked. I wanted to be like Jeanne. Beautiful.

One Friday evening, Jeanne set up an easel-like mirror in front of the TV. When she started pulling cosmetics from her trunk—compacts and pencils and blush—my sisters fumed.

on *Beauty*

They rolled their eyes. "Can't you do that somewhere else?" they cried out in unison.

Jeanne shrugged them off. "I have a date," she said.

While Jeanne carefully drew a line of blue over her eyelids, I leaned over to get a better view. I bumped her. The mirror toppled over. Jeanne smeared eyeliner on her face.

"What a klutz!" she exclaimed. Angry, she wiped the blue smudges off her face.

"You think you're so beautiful!" I yelled. Then I huffed off to my room.

After that night, I didn't watch *Wheel of Fortune* with my sisters anymore. I didn't want to sit next to Jeanne ever again. Instead, I retreated to my room, where I taught myself how to apply lipstick and file my nails. "What does Jeanne know about beauty?" I muttered

as I tried to flatten my bangs with hairspray and gel.

Much to my delight, by the time I turned sixteen I had finally filled out. My hair was longer, and thanks to a good orthodontist, my teeth were straight. "I'm not a klutz," I told myself, flipping my hair in front of the mirror.

Then something unthinkable happened to my oldest sister. Just before her high school graduation, Jeanne was severely injured in a car accident. After weeks in the hospital, she came home, hunched over on crutches and hobbling on a thick white cast. That evening my sisters guided her down the stairs to the rec room, and I helped her into an armchair.

Jeanne had stitches in her lips and bruises on her face. Her long hair hung limp. For a moment, my sisters and I stood around her chair in silence. It was hard to believe that this was Jeanne. Suddenly I knew what to do. "I'll get the curlers," I called out, already on my way to retrieve the makeup trunk from Jeanne's room.

My sisters began setting her hair, and I took a tube of eyeliner from the case. I waved it in front of Jeanne. "I know how to use it," I said. Jeanne's battered face broke into a smile. "I'm glad you still love me," she said. Her eyes were bright and shiny. Her smile was warm. Even though her face was scarred, Jeanne looked more beautiful than I'd ever seen her.

Ever so slowly, I etched a perfect line of blue over her eyelids. Thoughts filled my head and heart. *I've been searching for beauty in all the wrong places. The secret to beauty isn't found in a makeup trunk. It's what I'm seeing this very moment. . .a loveliness that comes from deep inside the heart.*

After I applied her makeup and my sisters rolled the last curler, we all pushed Jeanne's chair close to the TV. Grabbing floor pillows, we each took our places, once again encircling our oldest sister. Even though her cast blocked the screen, my sisters didn't seem to mind. Neither did I. *Wheel of Fortune* was on. And I was sitting next to Jeanne.

Beauty. . .should be that of your inner self, the unfading beauty of a gentle and quiet spirit, which is of great worth in God's sight.
1 PETER 3:3–4

Something We

That spring morning, my sister Lucy and I sat at the kitchen table, paging through Bibles and hymnals and prayer books. Our father had died the previous evening, and our mother had asked the two of us to plan his funeral.

I poured Lucy a cup of coffee. "I'm so glad you're here," I told her. Lucy offered a half smile, and I could tell we were feeling the same thing. Yet even though grief was welling up inside of us, we couldn't cry. There was no time for tears; we had work to do.

Lucy thumbed through her Bible, looking for appropriate readings for the service. "To everything there is a season...a time to be born...a time to laugh...a time to weep..." she read aloud.

I leaned over to skim the rest of the passage. "This verse, the one about laughing...it fits Dad," I said.

We began recalling the times in our childhood when Dad had made us laugh: the potato-sack races he organized on the Fourth of July, the jokes he told at the kitchen table, the off-key carols he sang at Christmastime.

We lingered over those memories for a moment in the quiet kitchen. I turned my glance back to Lucy's Bible. "A time to weep..." I repeated.

Lucy thought for a moment. "Dad wasn't much for tears," she said.

We reminisced about one Saturday morning when Dad had assigned yard

Needed to Do

chores to all nine of us kids. A former Navy officer, Dad measured six foot three and had shoulders like rocks. Wearing a baseball cap, he stood under a nearby oak tree with a clipboard, checking off our jobs.

Lucy was twelve and I was eleven, and we were to uproot dandelions while our siblings raked leaves and trimmed bushes. I knelt beside Lucy in the dirt and watched her furiously yank a weed from the garden and toss it into a bucket labeled: "Weeds——Lucy and Nancy."

"Dad won't let me go to the mall," she fumed, tears streaming down her face. I knew she had made plans to meet her junior high friends for lunch.

"Don't cry," I told her.

Just then, Dad came over to check on how many weeds were in our bucket. He saw Lucy crying. "Simmer down," he told her, his voice low and firm. "Simmer down." It was a familiar command, one that Dad often used to curtail our tears.

Around noon, Dad walked back to Lucy. He leaned down and patted her back. "Now you can go to the mall," he had said softly.

I poured Lucy another cup of coffee. "Dad loved you," I said.

Lucy nodded, and her eyes misted, but she resolutely

turned back to the books. "What about hymns?" she asked. For the rest of the day we busied ourselves with choosing songs, writing prayers, and designing a program. We didn't have time for tears. There was too much to do.

The next morning, Lucy and I met at the church an hour before the funeral. We mirrored each other with our black dresses and the dark circles under our eyes. The two of us sat on a bench overlooking the church lawn. Just then a little girl rode by on her bike.

"Remember the red bike?" Lucy said.

"How could I forget?"

On the morning of Lucy's thirteenth birthday, while she was still sleeping, I had watched Dad wheel a red bike into her room. It was a bargain he'd found at a garage sale. Beaming with expectation, Dad winked at me. "I spray painted the fenders," he said.

I wanted to say, "Dad, Lucy wanted a new bike," but I couldn't—I just couldn't. I peeked into Lucy's room just as her eyes fell upon the red bike, with its fat tires and a basket attached to the handlebars.

"Oh no!" Lucy wailed. She began sobbing, and her cries vibrated throughout the house. Dad hung his head. I waited for him to say, "That's enough…simmer down," but he didn't.

Now, so many years later, Lucy turned to me and asked, "When I was crying about the red bike…what did Dad say?"

I closed my eyes as I recalled Dad's words on that long-ago morning.

I looked at Lucy. "'Let her cry.' That's what Dad said…he said, 'Let her cry.'"

Lucy's eyes widened. "He did?"

I nodded and linked my arm in hers. And at that moment, we did something we both needed to do. We cried.

Sometimes you just need a hand to hold— and sisters know when.

PAM BROWN

A Psalm for My Sister

ADAPTED FROM PSALM 139

O Lord, You have searched my sister's heart.
You are familiar with all her ways.
You have laid Your hand upon her life;
she is blessed.
You created her; she is wonderfully made.
All her days were written in Your book,
even before she was born.
In infancy, You sent her to me.
Thank You for the days we have shared.

Throughout our years,
we have known Your constant presence.
You have gone behind us and before us;
You have seen our comings and our goings.
Has Your Spirit ever left us?

Even when we have shared
the darkest moments of life
and night has hemmed us in,
You have remained with us.
We are bound by the light of Your love.
How precious to us are Your thoughts,
how vast the sum of them.
We cannot grasp Your mind;
we cannot count Your thoughts.
Your knowledge is wonderful; it guides our lives.
O Lord, You have searched our hearts.
You are familiar with all our ways.
Your hand is upon us; Your hand made us sisters.
Forever we are blessed.

Teacup

It was Easter morning. The bright sun streamed into my grand-mother's dining room, where my sisters and I stood in front of a china hutch filled with teacups. The six of us were all under the age of twelve; we were wearing matching calico dresses and brimmed hats trimmed with long ribbons.

My grandmother, "Mema," placed a plate of warm cinnamon rolls on the table. She smiled as she saw us standing side by side, our hands pressed against the glass doors of the hutch. "Those are cups of love...priceless," she told us, her brown eyes twinkling behind her bifocals.

She explained that during the Great Depression she had received each second-hand cup as a gift from a friend or relative. We listened intently. We admired the patterns on the porcelain cups—every rose petal, each etching of emerald ivy, every silver-edged heart.

"I like the lavender cup…the one with the gold leaves," I said.

My sisters chimed in.

"My favorite is the one with the brass rim."

"Look at the blue one on the top shelf…"

Over the years, my sisters and I never tired of studying the sunlit cups in Mema's hutch. They were family treasures. The cups were part of Mema, part of us.

On my wedding day, I opened a small package wrapped in shiny white paper. Underneath a lacy bow, Mema had tucked a card. "Your favorite," it read. Inside was the lavender cup. My eyes misted. Even the finest china from Tiffany's couldn't compare.

When my sisters got married, they, too, received their favorite "cup of love." Mema has been gone now for many years, but my sisters and I still treasure the secondhand cups she called keepsakes. Now we proudly display the cups in our own homes.

On a recent Sunday morning, I hosted a family gathering at my house. After my sisters and I ate warm cinnamon rolls, we congregated around the hutch that holds my collection of teacups. One of my sisters pointed to the lavender cup trimmed with gold leaves. "There's Mema's cup."

I nodded, recalling the precious memories of Mema's love—memories that we, as sisters, will always hold in our hearts.

"It's a cup of love...priceless," I said.

I knew my sisters understood.

What greater thing is there for human souls than to feel that they are joined for life, to be with each other in silent, unspeakable memo[ries]

MARY ANN EVANS

Don't Ever Forget

I lay back in the dental chair, a huge wad of cotton in my mouth. The dentist had just yanked one of my upper molars, and he was in the next room writing me a prescription. I'm glad that's over, I told myself.

Earlier that morning, I had awakened in pain, my mouth throbbing from a toothache. I had to call several dentists before this one offered me an early appointment. Now from his tenth floor office, I looked out on the skyline of department stores, restaurants, and hotels.

When my gaze fixed on a towering brick building labeled Ridges Medical Center, I suddenly thought of my older sister, Kathy. *Pray for her*, an inner voice instructed. I quickly dismissed the prompting. Just a week earlier, I had seen Kathy at a family picnic. We had spent the afternoon talking about the soccer games our kids had won, ideas we had for decorating our homes, and the new outfits we had bought at bargain prices. Kathy told me how excited she was to be teaching a Bible study at her church. Everything was fine.

Still, the inner voice persisted: *Kathy needs your prayers. . . .*

I closed my eyes. Memories of my teenage years surfaced, and I saw myself at the age of sixteen. I was boarding a bus to Colorado, on my way to a Christian camp with my youth group. Before I climbed on the bus, Kathy handed me a Bible. "I want you to have this," she

said. On the front page, she had written a simple message: God loves you...don't ever forget that. That week God became a much bigger part of my life, and when I got back home, Kathy somehow knew that my faith had grown. "I'll be there for you," she told me. In the days that followed, my sister had guided me ever closer to God.

"Here's your prescription," the dentist said. "Try not to chew on that side." My pain forgotten, I grabbed the small slip of paper and headed for the elevator. I was already on my cell phone with my mother by the time the doors closed.

"Is Kathy okay?" I asked.

Mom sounded worried. "She's in the hospital. She's having a biopsy this morning. The doctors suspect cancer," she said.

I walked numbly through the lobby while Mom explained the seriousness of Kathy's condition.

"Which hospital?" I asked.

"Ridges. Ridges Hospital. Do you know where that is?"

Moments later, I stood in the hospital lobby. A gray-haired woman greeted me. "Your sister's being prepped for surgery," the receptionist said. "She can't have any visitors."

"May I write her a message?" I asked.

The woman smiled and handed me a sheet of hospital stationery and a silver pen. "I'll make sure your sister gets it before surgery," she said.

I began writing: *Dear Kathy...God sent me here...I have a message for you...God loves you...don't ever forget that....*

It's been about two years since that day in the hospital. Now, whenever I see Kathy at a family gathering, I'm reminded of the special bond we share. Common genes and a lifetime of memories connect us as sisters, but it is love—God's love—that will always bind our hearts.

While some sisters are kindred spirits from the beginning, I really began to appreciate my sister years later.

ALDA ELLIS

Picnic i

That Sunday afternoon, a snowstorm raged outside my mother's home. I was playing a game of Scrabble on the living room carpet with my kids, and Mom and Aunt Kate were sitting at the kitchen table. Sisters for over seventy years, the two of them were sifting through a box of family keepsakes.

Giggling like girls, they pulled faded black-and-white photos from the box, lingering over pictures that triggered special memories.

"Look at Mom on the farm...."

"There's one of you in my sweater...."

"That cheerleading outfit was always a little too tight for me...."

With one ear tuned to their conversation, I listened as they recounted family stories from the 1940s, tales of wartime and sacrifice.

he Snow

Aunt Kate handed my mother a yellowed piece of paper. "Here's the letter from Bud," she said. Tenderly, Mom ran her hand over the sixty-year-old note. Their nineteen-year-old brother had written it to both of them just a week before he was killed in World War II.

My mother read it aloud:

Dear Kate and Mary,

It will be swell to see my favorite sisters again. When I come home, we'll have a picnic in the park. We'll roast hot dogs and marshmallows....

Tears welled up in Aunt Kate's eyes. "We never had that picnic," she said, her voice quivering.

Mom stared at the letter. "We never got to say good-bye," she said softly.

They grew very quiet, and when I looked up from the Scrabble board, my eyes were drawn to the bookcase where Uncle Bud's picture was displayed. Dressed in a military uniform decorated with medals, he looked so young and confident. His eyes brown and bright, his cheekbones strong, Bud was a mirror that reflected the faces of my mom and aunt. Mom put the photos back into the box and then carefully tucked it into a nearby cabinet. Suddenly she turned to Aunt Kate and smiled. "We're gonna have that picnic," she announced.

"Now?" Aunt Kate asked.

"Now!" Mom declared. She opened a nearby hutch and pulled out a red-checkered tablecloth and spread it on the table.

The two of them rummaged through the freezer. Giggling in triumph, they pulled out a pack of hot dogs. They found a half-filled package of marshmallows in the cupboard and a bag of potato chips in the pantry. They laughed.

"But we don't have any buns," Aunt Kate said.

Mom grabbed a package of bread from the counter. "Yes, we do!" she said, waving the loaf in the air.

Mom and Aunt Kate set the table with paper plates and mustard. Then they bundled up in boots and scarves and coats, slid open the kitchen patio door, and made their way outside to the snow-covered deck. Mom brushed the snow from the grill and filled it with charcoal. Soon the two sisters stood in the snow, roasting hot dogs and marshmallows over a bright fire.

They motioned to me to join them. Grinning, I shook my head. This long overdue picnic was their time of love and laughter, of healing and letting go. This celebration of cherished memories was theirs and theirs alone. This was a moment that only sisters could share.

There are some memories best left deep within the crevices of the heart, surfacing only to answer the call of another kindred soul.

ANONYMOUS

Heart to Heart

❧ Give your sister her favorite pair of earrings from your jewelry collection.

CHOCOLATE
CHOCOLATE
CHOCOLATE

❧ Fill a basket with her favorite chocolates. Tuck in a handwritten poem or Scripture, rolled like a scroll and tied with a ribbon. Add a single flower and sprinkle with gold confetti.

Watch Chick Flicks

❧ Watch a sappy "chick flick" video together. Be sure you have a box of tissues and a big bowl of popcorn on hand.

❧ Go for a long walk together and stroll arm in arm.

Remember when...

❧ Throw a "Remember when..." party. Pass around old scrapbooks and photo albums.

Share your favorite growing-up stories. Let the laughter come...or even the tears.

Beauty Makeovers...

❧ Kidnap her and treat her to a beauty makeover. Double the fun by getting a makeover for yourself at the same time! Afterward, go out on the town for a fabulous dinner and celebrate yourselves!

❧ When she least expects it, call her. Tell her how much you love her.

Call her...

❧ Make a "sister collage." Arrange nostalgic momentos in a beautiful frame or shadow box. Include items like cherished photos, ticket stubs from shared events, sentimental cards or letters, and pieces of heirloom jewelry that hold special meaning to you both.

My sisters remain a constant in my life.

We share a history that lives on in the stories we tell and the memories we've stored in our hearts. Together we've learned to fight well and to forgive tenderly. Our ties of love are unbreakable. We are friends—forever friends.

Our lives are interconnected. When one of us hurts, we all feel pain. If joy touches one of our lives, our voices blend in a chorus of rejoicing. My sisters are part of me…. They will always be part of me.

I'm convinced that the sister relationship is a wondrous gift, one that deserves to be celebrated. Let's delight in the gift of sisters! Let's honor their unwavering support. Let's appreciate in a new way their constant presence in our lives.

Celebrate with your sister in a way that's unique to you. Throw a party. Bake her favorite treat. Make a huge sign that says: "I love my sister!" Write a poem praising her special qualities. Buy her some bubble bath. Have a picnic in the snow. Cheer for her. Cheer for the experiences you treasure, the memories you hold dear, and the dreams you will always share.

And while you're at it, send up a cheer to God—a cheer filled with gratitude for your sister. After all, this "sister thing" was His idea.

Thank you for always being there—entirely yourself and yet part of me.

PAM BROWN

to *Sisters*

Every good and perfect gift
is from above,
coming down from the Father
of the heavenly lights.
JAMES 1:17